spot

MIGHTY MACHINES

CRANES

by Mari Schuh

AMICUS | AMICUS INK

boom

cable

Look for these words and pictures as you read.

hook

load

A crane is ready to work.
What can it do?

A crane lifts heavy things.
It moves things side to side.

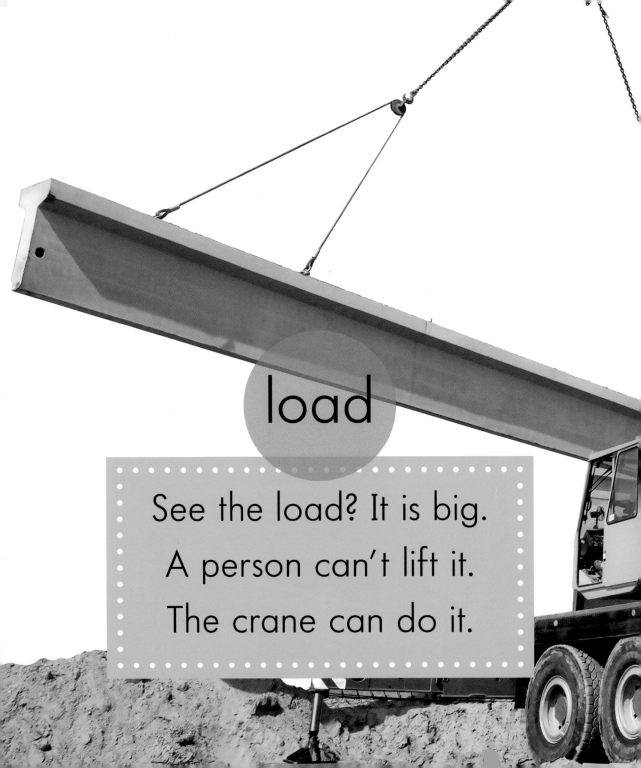

load

See the load? It is big.

A person can't lift it.

The crane can do it.

boom

See the boom?

It is a long arm.

It is made of steel.

See the cable?

It is a thick wire.

It is made of metal.

cable

See the hook?

It holds the load.

The hook has a latch.

hook

Here is a new building.

A crane lifts a long beam.

Up it goes!